Lights, Camera, Action!

A Fun Look at the Movies

by Anita Higman

Perfection Learning® CA

Cover Illustration: Michael A. Aspengren

To Scott and Hillary: My heart's desire was to have children.
Thank you for being my dreams come true!

About the Author

Anita Higman grew up on a farm in Oklahoma. She loved catching catfish in a nearby creek. But she wasn't very good at it. One time, her pole came flying up. And her fish landed in a tree! She hasn't given up though. She still enjoys fishing whenever her family will trust her with a pole!

While growing up, Anita also liked reading poetry and mystery novels. And she enjoyed playing with words as the editor of her high school newspaper.

Mrs. Higman now has five books with four more coming out. She lives in Texas with her husband and two children.

Acknowledgments

My appreciation goes to Grammy award-winning singer and actress Darlene Koldenhoven for her wonderful answers to my questions about the movie business.

Many thanks go to Tom and Janet Townsend for their help with the "Bring in the Tanks" chapter.

Much gratitude goes to animal trainer Renee C. Toth for her fun visit about animals in the movies.

And a big thank you to actor Gordon Williams for his help and his interesting comments about being an extra.

I would also like to express my appreciation to Andrea Ricks for her suggestions.

Please Take Note

The guns mentioned in this book are for the movies. But even these fake guns can be deadly. Remember, guns, weapons, and explosives are not toys. They can kill.

Also, the mention of certain movies in this book does not necessarily constitute an endorsement by the author or the publisher.

Image credits: Art Today pp. 36, 39, 41, 42 (middle), 44, 50; Annie Griffiths Belt/Corbis p. 14; Brigitte Jouxtel pp. 6, 18; Museum of Modern Art/Film Stills Archive pp. back cover, 9, 16, 34, 42 (top, bottom); Tom Townsend pp. 27, 28, 31, 32; Gordon Williams p. 22.

For information, contact
Perfection Learning® Corporation, 1000 North Second Avenue,
P.O. Box 500, Logan, Iowa 51546-0500
Phone: 1-800-831-4190 • Fax: 1-800-543-2745
perfectionlearning.com
Paperback ISBN 0-7891-2866-7
Cover Craft® ISBN 0-7807-7837-5

Table of Contents

Roll 'Em!

Picture this. It's cozy and dark. Your chair is soft. You're stuffing yourself silly with buttery popcorn. You're slurping up an ice-cold soda.

And then—that second you've been waiting for—the movie begins!

The silver screen comes to life with all your favorite actors. They make you chuckle. Sometimes you cry. Or you grip the armrests during the nonstop action.

Well, it took a lot of work to make it all happen that way.

Did you ever watch a movie and wonder how an actor got the part? Did you wonder how they got an animal to do all those tricks?

Movies involve a lot of make-believe. They take a lot of hard work. That's what makes it look real.

Let's go on an adventure. We'll explore a few back roads of the movie business.

An actress will tell us how people get into films. There's a wacky movie script. And you'll get a bunch of information about this thing called—

THE MOVIES!

Celebrity Talk
The Inside Scoop!

Sometimes Hollywood movie **roles** come by surprise. That has happened to at least one person in Hollywood. Her name is Darlene Koldenhoven. She sings for commercials and movies. Now she acts too!

A movie company hired her for music coaching. She ended up being one of the singing nuns in the movies *Sister Act* and *Sister Act 2: Back in the Habit.* She has also been in two other movies.

Darlene also does vocal work for the movies. She has sung on and off camera for some popular movies. They include *Free Willy, Apollo XIII, Home Alone,* and *Home Alone 2: Lost in New York.*

Darlene has many **talents.** She sings **backup** for famous musical artists. She has even won a **Grammy** award. This is a major award in the music business.

She's a recording artist too. So she has her own music out on CDs.

Darlene has always wanted to sing. She began performing at age three. At 19, she sang solo with a famous symphony orchestra.

Darlene sings in an amazing five-**octave** range. This means that she can sing very high notes, low notes, and everything in between.

Darlene moved to California after college. She gave piano lessons. And soon, people noticed what a great musician she is.

Darlene is easy to talk to. It's like visiting with your best friend. I enjoyed learning more about how the movie business works. Here's a peek at our showbiz talk.

Interview

Question: Will you be trying for more movie roles?

Answer: Sure. I always have my **demo** tape ready. And my feelers are out there. But the type of roles I always go for are musically oriented. There aren't many of those out there.

Question: Do you think you'll ever go for the nonsinging roles?

Answer: If something comes up, yes. I do enjoy the acting too. It's another type of expression.

Question: Is acting fun?

Answer: Yes. But it's a lot of hard work too.

Question: I know you do on-camera work. What is that?

Answer: In on-camera work, I'm seen in the movie.

Question: And you also do off-camera work? What is that?

Answer: I'm not seen in off-camera work. Only heard. I might be the singing voice of another actress. Or I might be part of a choir that can be heard singing. Also, we don't always sing words. Many times our voices are used as an instrument. You may only hear "oohs" and "ahs."

Question: How did your first movie vocal job go?

Answer: It went well. I had an off-camera job. Someone else couldn't make it. They called me at the last minute. They asked me to sing a **score** full of eerie-sounding notes for a scary movie. The strange notes I sang seemed to be picked out of the air. So my first job was the hardest. But I'm glad I did it. It went well. Doors began to open for me in the business.

7

Question: Did you have many **contacts** when you first started?

Answer: No. And that's unusual. There are a lot of people in this business who have relatives already working in the movies. This helps pave the way for them.

I had none of that. In fact, when I moved out here, all my belongings were stolen. So I started in the business with almost nothing.

Question: So you struggled at first?

Answer: Yes. I had trouble getting started. I sang **classical** and religious music growing up. So I worked as a music teacher.

When I came to Hollywood, I really didn't know what I wanted to do. When I arrived, I didn't know anything about self-promotion. I didn't know anything about getting an **agent.** Or how to get work. I had to figure it out on my own.

Question: So what did you do?

Answer: I decided to teach piano. I put up signs all over the place. Even in grocery stores. After a while, I began teaching piano to movie stars' children. Then I heard about a contact I could make. That led to my first singing job.

Question: What do you mean when you say "self-promotion"?

Answer: Your talent is like a product. It's like a box of cereal. You have to let other people know about your product. And try to sell it. Whether it's acting, singing, or another talent. You are constantly talking to people about what you do. And what your skills are. You have to present yourself in a way that isn't conceited. But in a way that is confident.

Question: What can young people do to get started in this business?

Answer: There are so many different parts to this business. Not just acting. You might decide you want to be the electrician who works on the movies.

But first, do some research. Read magazine articles.

 9

Talk to people in the business. Find out what skills are needed for different jobs. Figure out what you are good at. Then ask yourself, "Do I have the right personality to handle this business? Can I handle promoting myself all the time?"

Question: Do you take all the jobs that come along?

Answer: No. But I do take most of the jobs. This is a very social business. Usually, one job leads to the next. But there are jobs I've turned down. I felt they didn't go along morally with my belief system.

Question: What area of music did you win your Grammy award in?

Answer: I won it for jazz vocal performance by a group.

Question: How can a person win a Grammy?

Answer: The record is submitted to the National Academy of Recording Arts and Sciences. The members of the recording group listen to each work. Then they vote for the best in each category.

Question: What does it feel like to have your name called at the Grammy Awards? And have hundreds of people applaud as you walk on stage to accept your award?

Answer: I was very thankful. It felt good to win. When I heard the applause, it was like people were saying thank you for all my hard work.

Question: Do you hope to someday win an **Academy Award?**

Answer: There are two ways of looking at awards. It's a nice way of saying thank you to people for their hard work. But there are many people who don't get the award who deserved it just as much. I like receiving awards. But I don't go to sleep thinking, "I've got to have that award."

Question: Is the movie business hard to break in to?

Answer: It's very hard.

Question: Why is that?

Answer: Because there are just too many people trying to get jobs in the movies. It's a very **competitive** business. The people in **casting** may go through a thousand pictures and **résumés** to find someone for a movie role.

Question: Do you like **auditions?**

Answer: I don't like the audition process. But I do enjoy the challenge of the work.

Question: Why?

Answer: I'll get a call. They'll say, "Can you come this afternoon?" You have to rush around to get there on time. Then you wait a lot.

When it's your turn, you stand in front of a camera. People ask you to state your name. And then they ask you to do your thing. You are only allowed a few moments for the tryout. Then they say, "Thank you very much. Good-bye. Make sure you leave your picture and résumé."

That's pretty much the way an audition goes.

Question: What advice do you give kids who want to get into this business?

Answer: First of all, don't think you have to be in the movies. Your life isn't over if you don't make it in a movie. There are plenty of satisfying experiences you can get performing in your community theater. There are so many fulfilling things you can do with your talents. You can still feel developed as a person. Even if you're not the star in a movie.

Question: Do you have any advice for people who plan to go to Hollywood?

Answer: I think you should first make it big in your own community. Get some good things on your résumé before you come. Do that before you try to tackle Hollywood. It may make it easier to break into the business. And ask yourself, "Do I have the kind of personality that can deal with the pressures of Hollywood? Do I mind constantly looking for more work?"

Question: Do you have to live in L.A. to be in this business?

Answer: To be in the big-time movies, it helps to live either in L.A. or New York. It helps especially to live in L.A.

Question: Did you always want to do this?

Answer: Yes. I've known I'd be a singer since age three. I had a knack for performing. So I did a lot of it growing up. I was the kid in the neighborhood who said, "Let's do a little show." I'd clean out the garage. I'd set up shelves and drape sheets over it. I'd make a stage. Then we'd make up characters and do a puppet show.

Question: Did you perform as you got older?

Answer: Yes. I got my first lead role in a musical in the ninth grade. I jumped into whatever production they were doing. I performed in college as well.

Question: What helped you decide to become a performer?

Answer: My teachers in school showed me I had talent. Also, my mother putting me onstage at age three helped me want to perform.

Question: Do you like what you do?

Answer: Yes. I love what I do.

Question: Why?

Answer: Because I am using the gifts that were given to me. I guess you could say I'm not working against the grain.

Question: Describe a typical morning on a movie set.

Answer: Well, you get up at 4:30 in the morning. You get on a bus. It goes from the hotel to the movie set. First, you may have your hair and makeup done. Or you eat breakfast. Then you go to the set. They **block** the scene. The camera people and the director discuss the lighting and the movement of the characters. After that scene is rehearsed, there's a break.

Question: What happens when people are late?

Answer: It's difficult when people don't show up on time. Everyone has to wait on them. That slows everything down. Movies cost a lot of money to make. And it's important that people act responsibly.

Question: Do people get angry?

13

Answer: Yes. Sometimes tempers flare easily. A lot of money is at stake. Everyone feels the pressure to get it right the first time.

Question: What is a *stand-in?*

Answer: Each main actor will usually have one. This is someone who's about the same size and coloring as the actor.

The stand-in will stand in the actor's place. Then adjustments are made by the camera and lighting crew. That way, the star's energy isn't wasted just standing around waiting.

Question: Is that another job people can do to get started?

Answer: Yes. That's another job. You might say, "Well, you're only the stand-in." But the stand-in is on the set. They get to talk to a lot of people. Even the director. That's what you need to succeed in this business. You have to have one-on-one contact with as many people as you can.

Question: Do you make friends?

Answer: Yes. I do. But some people are real friends. And others are just people you get to know in the business. There aren't enough hours in a day to make everyone your best friend. I would love to. But many times, I don't even get to see my singing and acting friends. I am always out meeting a lot of new people. Sometimes that's hard to deal with.

Question: Is it hard to have a lot of friends in this business?

Answer: It's best to find one or two people to be your dear friends. But even then, it's hard sometimes. This business is very competitive. And your best friend may end up taking your job. So you may even lose your best friend.

Question: Let's talk about when somebody steals a job from you. How do you handle that?

Answer: You can try to talk to the person. You can kindly ask about his or her behavior. But it's a touchy situation. Generally, I just turn the other cheek. That means you just let it go and don't worry about it.

Question: Do you think being famous is important?

Answer: No. It's not important for your own personal happiness.

Question: Does fame bring money?

Answer: Not always. People assume I'm rich because I've won a Grammy. But I'm a working woman like everybody else.

They do pay millions when you are a star in a movie. But personally, I think they have

 15

everything backward. I think that teachers should be paid millions. And some of the stars and sports figures could do a little more with their money for other people. Thankfully, many of them do.

Question: Who are your favorite actors?

Answer: Probably Mel Gibson and Meryl Streep.

Question: What's one of your favorite movies?

Answer: Actually, I loved the movie *Sister Act*. And not just because I was in it. It was a feel-good movie. And it had a great message.

Question: Do you go to a lot of movies?

Answer: I like movies. And I go when I have the time. But I have to try not to analyze the whole thing. I just try to enjoy it.

Question: Is it easier in this business if you have a variety of talents?

Answer: Yes. It's good to have many skills in this business. It will give you a better chance to make a living at it. But you have to be really good at all those skills. If you get an agent, they will have you fill out a form. They'll want to know all the talents you have. Do you rollerblade? Do you ride a horse? You check everything you can do. The more you have, the better. That agent may then call needing an actor who also sings. Or one who can skateboard during a scene.

Question: Is it easy to get an agent?

Answer: No. It's hard to get an agent unless you have a job. And it's hard to get a job without an agent. That's called a *Catch-22*. But it can be done. In my case, I got a job first. And then I got an agent.

Question: What are some of the things agents do?

Answer: They try to set an actor up with auditions. If the actor gets the role, they work out the **contract** for you. And how much money you'll get paid.

Question: How do agents get paid?

Answer: They get paid part of the money the actor made on that job.

Question: Do you think an actor should try to get an agent?

Answer: It can help a lot to have an agent.

Question: Is graduating from high school important to an actor?

Answer: Yes. It's very important.

Question: Do you think movies are like real life?

Answer: No.

Question: Did you get scared performing when you were growing up?

Answer: No. Performing just seemed fun to me.

Question: Do you ever get scared now?

Answer: I rarely get scared. If I do, it's because I didn't

prepare enough. Still sometimes it happens. Then I'll forget the lyrics when I'm singing.

Question: Have you ever forgotten the words to a song when you're performing?

Answer: Yes. When I do forget, I just make up new words to the song as I'm singing. You have to learn to be quick and creative. And actors do the same thing when they forget their lines. In fact, most actors have taken a course in *improvisation*.

Question: What is that?

Answer: It's a class for actors where you make things up as you go. You learn how to think quickly on your feet. How to interact with other actors on the spur of the moment. And it helps build your creative sense.

Question: Do other actors get scared when they perform?

Answer: Yes. Some of them.

Question: How do they get over it?

Answer: Some stars never get over stage fright. They just go out there and get sweaty palms. And they just get through it by focusing on their work.

Question: What's the largest group of people you've ever performed live for?

Answer: Over 40,000 people. But it doesn't matter how may people there are. I would give the same performance for five people. Because I believe in excellence.

Question: Why do you think movies are so popular?

Answer: Because I think visual impressions are the strongest and most lasting.

Question: Could movies be too powerful in people's lives?

Answer: Yes, if people start acting out the bad things they see on the screen. And if they let Hollywood movies be their guide in life. Then they're giving movies too much power. There are good movies and bad movies. It's important to learn the difference.

Question: Do you still have new things to learn?

Answer: Oh, yes! I wish there were more than 24 hours in a day. Because I love learning things. It's my favorite thing to do. I am like a sponge. To me, learning about anything excites me.

Question: Did you enjoy school?

Answer: I liked the learning part. But I had a hard time with the competition and the **cliques.** It's not fun to be rejected by a group.

Question: Do you enjoy reading books?

Answer: I love reading. I have hundreds of books of all kinds.

Question: Has reading books helped you in your business?

Answer: Yes! There are books on acting and how to get an agent. How to do an audition. Even how to do children's auditions. There are books for just about everything.

Question: Do you have any other great tips for people who want to get into this business?

Answer: Get a good education. Read books. Be prepared. Practice a lot. Be kind to everyone. Be positive. Learn to speak for yourself with confidence. But also with humility. That means that you should talk about yourself without bragging. And if you do go for it, keep at it. Don't give up.

Question: Great answers, Darlene! Just for fun, would you please give us your autograph?

Answer: I'd be happy to!

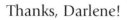

Thanks, Darlene!

2

Cattle Call
Talking to a Movie Extra

Gordon Williams loves stage acting. He's performed in 90 stage productions.

But he's also been in a number of films. Sometimes he's offered speaking parts. Many times, he's an *extra*. This is a person who has a small nonspeaking part in a movie.

Gordon enjoys historical epics. He saw one at age 13. That hooked him.

He then wanted to read more history. And that made him want to become an actor.

Here's Gordon. He'll tell you about being an extra.

Hi there. I'm Gordon Williams. Yes, I've been an extra many times. I am also a clerk.

I love acting. But I have to work another job too. In fact, most actors must do that. Because sometimes acting doesn't pay well. I also make extra money by doing commercials and plays.

There are different ways to become an extra. I looked in the newspaper for a *cattle call.* This funny term means "a request for actors."

Gordon Williams

Here's how this experience went:

I went to the hotel where they held the cattle call. The casting staff snapped a picture of me. They wanted my phone number, address, and other information.

They even needed to know my measurements. In case the wardrobe staff needed to fit me for a costume.

A week later, they called me in the evening. The casting director asked if I could be there the next morning for the shoot. The shoot is the actual filming of the movie.

The casting director holds an important job. She's in charge of getting the right actors and extras for the film. But job titles and responsibilities can change. It depends on how big the production is.

Once there, I spent most of my time waiting. A long time passed before they called me onto the set. The set is a place where everything is set up to shoot the scene.

My part was simply to walk past the star of the movie. I was paid very little to do this.

Being an extra isn't very glamorous. But it gave me some experience in the movie business. And that's what I wanted.

 I've heard that working on a movie is like working a jigsaw puzzle. That's because some of the scenes are filmed in different places. And they usually shoot the scenes out of order.

In one scene, the director spent 25 hours shooting. Out of that, he only got five minutes of the movie completed! They make it all look so easy. But a lot happens behind the camera.

As an extra, I've played different roles. I've played a policeman, a tailor, a security guard, and a janitor. A number of times I've simply been part of a crowd.

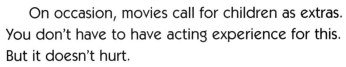

 Sometimes, I've ended up on the cutting room floor. That means my part wasn't used in the movie after all. It got edited out, or cut, for one reason or another. That can happen to an actor with a speaking part too.

On occasion, movies call for children as extras. You don't have to have acting experience for this. But it doesn't hurt.

If you want acting experience, try doing community theater. Or get involved in a local church drama production.

How about the school drama club? Take advantage of every acting opportunity you can. There's no one right way to do this.

But remember, not all movies are good to be in. In fact, I turned down some jobs because I thought they had bad moral content. I like to feel good about the movies I'm in.

I want to become a very fine actor. That is one of my goals. I also hope to have more speaking roles in the future.

Two actor favorites of mine are George C. Scott and Charlton Heston. They are my heroes as performers.

If you want to get into the movie business, here's some advice—

First, make sure it is something you really love. I don't think you should become an actor because of the money. Or because you think it is the "in" thing.

Usually, people in this business are either overpaid or underpaid. Most of us are underpaid.

And it's good to do many different things. An actor may have to do commercials and stage plays as well as movies to make a living.

Just remember to go for it for the right reasons. And then do your best!

Gordon's Top 10 Acting Tips

Have you ever wanted to act? Have you always dreamed of being an actor?

Gordon has been acting for 32 years. Here are some of the lessons he's learned.

1. You don't have to be outgoing to become an actor.
2. Anybody can memorize lines if you repeat them enough.
3. Do your homework. Know your lines.
4. Be on time for **rehearsals** and performances.
5. Be on your best behavior. Respect the director. Give your very best. Even if you're not the star of the show.
6. Be considerate of the other actors as well as the crew members. They also have important jobs to do.
7. Part of being a good actor is being a good listener. During the rehearsals, learn to listen to your fellow actors.
8. Give your best all the time. Even when you're not getting paid.
9. Get as much acting experience as you can.
10. Learn to **discipline** yourself. Acting is like sports. You have to exercise and practice.

You may have to get up early in the morning to be at practice. If you want something badly enough, then there is a price you have to pay. But it's worth it in the end.

Bring in the Tanks

Have you ever seen a movie about the military? Have you seen a movie about a war? Ever wondered where they get all that equipment? How could they round up all those tanks and guns and gear?

Well, they may have gotten it from a man like Tom Townsend. Tom rents military equipment to the movie business. Tom is also an author, a producer of low-budget films, and a friend of mine.

Let's see what Tom has to say about his part in the film industry. I think you'll find it very interesting!

My father was in the army. I grew up on military bases all over the world. I have great respect for our armed forces. I guess I'm interested in military gear because I spent so much time around it when I was a kid.

As an adult, I started collecting combat vehicles and other items. It was just a hobby. Then I decided to turn this expensive hobby into a business.

I offer many kinds of vehicles to the movie industry. I actually own some of them. I keep those parked in my barn. I have several Jeeps from different periods in history. And I own a Ferret

Armored Car. This vehicle is like a small tank. But it has wheels instead of treads. It's meant to be fast, low, and quiet.

I also have a Bren Carrier (a British vehicle) and many others. I also supply whatever must go with the vehicle. Examples are drivers, gunners, and radio operators.

I also rent out weapons systems, guns, and military **props.** The weapons systems are a part of the vehicle. For example, the Ferret Armored Car has a machine gun mounted in it. It also fires smoke grenades. And it has a submachine gun and two pistols inside.

In the U.S., you don't need a license to drive a tank. But I do train my drivers. A tank is fun to operate. But it's difficult to move around.

You can't take a tank out on the freeway. Tanks have treads on them. Some of them can weigh around 50 tons. They will chew up the road as they go. So we transport them on trucks.

Sometimes, a movie needs a vehicle that we don't have. So we give a "makeover" to one we do have. We can make the vehicle look like it fits the period. And the location.

This process is called *VISMOD*. It's a short word for "visual modification."

We might take one vehicle and cover it. Perhaps with sheet metal, plywood, or fiberglass. We will change it to make it look and act like another vehicle.

I bought my vehicles from private collectors. These people had bought the vehicles from the government.

Combat vehicles are expensive. They can cost as much as a new car.

The guns I rent are not real. They fire blanks or another form of fake gunfire. We never use real bullets.

Remember, guns and weapons are not toys. They can kill people. Even blanks in guns can be dangerous. Blanks can be deadly if a person is too close to the gun when it is fired. Care has to be taken on the movie set so no one gets hurt.

I also provide military props such as belts, canteens, and ammo pouches. One unusual prop I own is a World War II portable airport beacon. I even have different models of rocket launchers. Of course, these are all fake. But we can make them look like they fire.

Another aspect of my business is supplying *reenactors*. These people are historians. And they're military collectors. They have their own uniforms and weapons for a particular period in history.

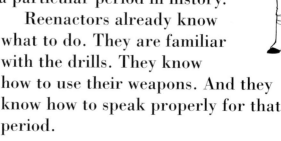

Reenactors already know what to do. They are familiar with the drills. They know how to use their weapons. And they know how to speak properly for that period.

The actors need very little training. If you hire 100 reenactors, you've created an instant army.

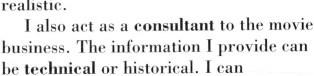

Many of these performers are very talented. They get paid about two to three times what an extra gets paid. They help make a movie look more realistic.

I also act as a **consultant** to the movie business. The information I provide can be **technical** or historical. I can answer questions about most periods in military history.

I got most of this knowledge from reading books. I can tell a director what kind of vehicles and uniforms they should have for a given period.

For instance, what should they use in a scene set in West Germany? Perhaps during the Cold War in 1956?

The director may ask me if they are correct when setting up a scene. It may be that he's half right.

Then I would suggest changes. And I might have to say that it will cost more money if he wants to be totally correct. That's just some of what I do in consulting.

Along with two other people, I have started a production company. We will be producing low-budget films. Our specialty will be historical **documentaries.**

We are now editing our first film, *Operation Pacific Fury*. It is a reenactment of some battle scenes from World War II.

We are also starting another new business. My wife, Janet, and I would like to provide **mythical** beasts for the film industry.

We own miniature cows. One is a miniature Highland cow. Ours may be one of the smallest Highland cows in the world. This cow is only 36 inches high. And it is fully grown.

It could have a **prehistoric** appearance with some simple and safe changes. With some extra hair, it could even look like a woolly mammoth!

Someone may want to set a movie on another planet. This tiny cow might be just right to portray a beast that has never existed. With makeup, it could look human-like or teddy bear-like. This unique cow would be perfect for science fiction or fantasy films.

We also raise miniature horses. They are about 29 inches high.

They've been trained in performance classes. And we are working on fitting them with realistic lightweight horns on their specially built halters. This will create the **illusion** that the horses are unicorns.

These animals will all do well. Especially when a movie needs a live beast that doesn't look like anything else. It's much cheaper to use makeup and fake horns than to build and **animate** these animals.

Janet and I have fun with our tiny pet cows and horses. They are expensive. But they are fun to raise and take care of. They eat out of our hands. And they like to follow us around too!

Well, maybe that gives you some insight into what I do for films. Hope to see you at the movies!

4

Animals in the Movies

It's a Zoo Out There!

Now here's an unusual job! Meet Renee Toth. She trains animals for the movies. And she is an animal talent agent. She helps other people's animals work in the movie business.

Renee also trains animals to perform in TV commercials. She's been having a great time with this unique career for 14 years.

They call Renee an animal wrangler. She told me all this super-fun stuff about the business.

Have you ever watched a movie where a cat leaps from a windowsill? Or butterflies flit away? Or someone wrestles an alligator? It means there's an *animal wrangler* on the movie set.

Animal wranglers are hired to bring in whatever animals or insects are needed for the movie. And to help them do their jobs.

 33

An animal might be considered background. Background, or dressing, is when you see a dog sleeping on a porch. Or when you see pretty swans swimming by.

An animal could be a *featured animal*. A featured animal has a special part in a film. In the movie *Free Willy*, the whale was a featured animal.

Renee usually brings her own equipment to the set. But sometimes the movie staff helps her.

Renee keeps some animals at her home. She trains them there. She even has a pet spider monkey in her house. She's named Rita. Renee sometimes dresses her monkey in a little safari outfit.

Rita will be in the movies someday too. But right now, Rita enjoys making a lot of mischief.

Renee also has access to many different kinds of animals. She told me all about her contacts. She can bring animals in from all over the world.

Renee said, "I have worked with all kinds of animals. A few of them are elephants, giraffes, camels, bears, tigers, lions, cougars, and snakes. I have even worked with a *wallaby.* A wallaby is like a small kangaroo.

"And of course, I work with dogs, cats, birds, and farm animals."

She can get almost any animal for the movies. But the koala bear is hard to find. Renee is careful to only supply animals that are legal to bring into the U.S.

Renee told me that many people think their own pets are perfect for the movies. But that isn't always true.

For instance, some cats will perform only at home. An indoor cat may change its personality outside. And some dogs might become shy in front of the cameras. They might be bothered by the noise and activity.

Renee uses animals that aren't scared of strangers, bright lights, or the *boom mike*. That's a microphone on a pole that hangs just above the actors. This is done so no one will see the mike on the screen.

The boom mike can frighten a dog. Or the dog may think it's a fuzzy toy and want to play. So it's easier to work with animals that are used to being around movie equipment.

Usually, Renee must *prep*, or prepare, an animal before it can be in a movie, even if it's trained well.

For example, the animal might need to do something unique to the movie like running from spot A to spot B. Renee would make sure the animal could do it.

Renee doesn't always use trained animals. Sometimes, the actions she needs come naturally to an animal. She just has to find a way to bring out that behavior.

Renee said that she sometimes gives the animals something positive such as their favorite foods or a toy. This will encourage the animal to perform.

Renee has to stay creative when working with animals. She must come up with quick answers to problems.

Renee shared some of her secrets with me. Take a look at what she said.

Sometimes I need lizards for a shoot. I keep them cool when I want them to slow down. This will make them easier for an actor to hold.

To make them active again, I place them under a heat lamp.

I use pigeons a lot. I get homing pigeons. Homing pigeons always go back home. That way we don't have to worry about them getting lost.

Sometimes I need a bird to settle down. I simply cover its eyes. It then becomes calm. For a bird, the saying "Out of sight, out of mind" is really true.

One time, I needed crows for my work. But I didn't have them. So I brought in some doves instead. I covered their wings with black coloring. It was washable and safe for their feathers. From a distance, they looked like real crows!

Sometimes, I need to do a scene where the pigeons are supposed to stay in the area. I then gently tape their wings. I use a safe and removable tape that doesn't hurt the bird.

Also, I can cut Ping-Pong balls in half. I paint these to look like pigeon heads. I place these gently on the heads of the pigeons. **They can't see anything.** So they will stay calm. And they won't fly away.

But I am always watching out for the animals. I want to make sure they are safe and happy. I would never do anything to harm animals. I see the animals I work with as my friends.

Renee said that she once had nine large cats. And she meant *large*.

She owned lions, leopards, a cougar, and a tiger. She rescued these animals.

Renee commented, "It has been popular for people to buy these animals. These cats are cute when they're cubs.

"But a big problem arises when they grow up! People don't realize how much work they are. Or how dangerous they can be. It doesn't work well to have a tiger in most backyards. Or a lion in your apartment. You still have to have a healthy respect for these animals."

For a while, Renee took in these huge cats because people no longer wanted them. She took good care of them. And many of them got to be in the movies.

Renee said that dogs are very popular in the movies. Most of the dogs she uses compete in dog shows. Some competitions require dogs to go through a series of obstacles. These animals have been trained well. And they are easier to use in the movies. They can do a series of *behaviors,* or trained actions. To a trainer, these behaviors are the things the animals can do on command.

For example, let's say that the dog is supposed to scratch—because he has fleas.

That is a behavior. It may be a trick for the dog. But it appears as a behavior to the audience.

Renee talks about her own dog:

One of my favorite animals to work with is my own terrier dog. I call him Action Jackson. He's smart. And he has many behaviors. He can do them over and over. That is, once he figures out what I want him to do.

Action Jackson yawns and sneezes on command. He can cover his nose and hide his head. And he'll go to a mark on command.

I can take the behaviors he has and mix them together. This makes it easier to create what they need in a scene.

I've had Action Jackson since he was eight weeks old. So I know what he can do. I know how to get him motivated. I know when he is too tired. Or when he is overheated. I like using him. It's easier to work with him. Because I know him so well.

If you want your dog to come to you, try squatting. The squatting puts you on his level. Then clap your hands. This is a good way to get your dog to come back to you.

If you want your dog to learn tricks, try an obedience class. But you should go to the class too. Then you can learn how to train your dog. It is good for your dog to be with other dogs in the class. It makes him friendlier with other animals.

Renee told me most movies use animals or insects. Sometimes you don't even notice them. They are in the background. But they are usually there. And that means there is an animal wrangler there to help them do their job.

Renee even worked with cockroaches. It was the only time she didn't adore her work. She said, smiling, "I would much rather work with snakes than roaches. But it was my job. And I jumped only once on the set!"

Renee can even work with butterflies. Once, she had the chrysalises sent to her home. The *chrysalis* is a stage in the butterfly's life. It's still in its cozy cocoon.

Renee made a special place for the chrysalises. Then they all began to hatch. Hundreds of them! She was a busy mom!

She fed them red sugar water. Renee continued to care for the butterflies. Then during the filming, they were all set free. Working with butterflies was one of the most unique requests she's had. It was one of the most fun too.

Renee said that in a way, she'd trained for this job since she was a girl. She loved animals. She was the kid who wanted to bring every animal home.

She even snatched up a lizard on a family vacation. She carried him home. And she took good care of him.

But she doesn't recommend that other kids do this. Because it might be a reptile that is poisonous or one that bites!

But the point is, she started slowly with this business. And now training animals is her full-time job!

Renee also had something to say about job choices.

I think people get locked into careers. You shouldn't always think you must have a typical career.

You might see a dog in the movies. But you may not know there is a job behind it. Maybe you didn't even know about a career like mine. Just remember, there are many different kinds of careers out there. I took the talents I had. And then I made up my own job. And boy, do I like that job!

Thanks, Renee. We enjoyed the visit.

Fun Movie Facts

1. Many people were a part of the invention of movies. Thomas Edison and his assistant, W. K. L. Dickson, became part of this process. They invented the kinetoscope in the 1890s.

   This machine showed very short films. But they were seen by just one person at a time. A person would insert a coin. Then he or she stared through a lens to see moving images. Thomas Edison didn't really think people would want to watch these films in a group.

2. The Lumiere brothers from France saw the kinetoscope device. But these two inventors thought that people *would* want to see films in groups. So the Lumiere brothers invented the cinematograph. With this new machine, movies could be viewed by entire audiences.

3. The first movies made for the theater were silent films. They had no sound.

4. The first movies with sound were called *talkies*.

THE BURGLAR'S DILEMMA

THE BOY, HAVING PAID THE PRICE FOR HIS OFFENCE IS HELPED TO BREAK WITH THE OLD LIFE AND REHABILITATE HIMSELF

5. The first feature-length movie with some sound was *The Jazz Singer*. Al Jolson was the star of the film. It came out in 1927.

6. The first science fiction movie was *A Trip to the Moon*. It came out in 1902.

7. One of the first stars of the cinema was actress Lillian Gish.

8. Charlie Chaplin was one of the first great comedians of the cinema. He directed movies as well. He created a famous silent-film character known as the "Little Tramp."

9. The movie *Gone with the Wind* was released in 1939. It was a big hit. And it made a lot of money. This movie was based on a novel by Margaret Mitchell. The novel was set during the Civil War. It was a bestseller. The two main characters were Scarlett O'Hara and Rhett Butler. The actors who played these roles were Vivien Leigh and Clark Gable.

10. *Citizen Kane* is considered a classic. It is in black-and-white. It was released in 1941. Orson Welles directed it. He starred in it too. Some people think it is one of the best films ever made.

11. Stan Laurel and Oliver Hardy (Laurel and Hardy) were a comedy team. They starred in many popular movies together.

12. Back in 1948, you could buy a movie ticket for 40 cents!

13. Cecil B. DeMille was a famous American filmmaker in earlier movie days. One of his historical epics was *The Ten Commandments*.

14. Today, Steven Spielberg is a popular American filmmaker. One of his famous films is *E.T. The Extra-Terrestrial*.

15. A movie script is a *screenplay*.

16. A movie can be shot on a set built at the studio. Or it can be shot *on location*. That means it's shot outside the studio. For example, a beach scene could be shot on location—at a real beach.

17. You've seen the *credits*. That's the list of people who were in the movie. The list also includes other people who have helped with the movie, like the director and the producer. It also includes the special effects people and the makeup staff. You can see the full list of credits at the end of each movie.

Imaginations Unlimited

A Wacky Little Screenplay

Have you ever wondered how a movie becomes a movie? It all starts with an idea. That's how almost everything starts. Right?

The idea is written in a script form. This is called a *screenplay*. The screenplay can be an original story. Or it can be an **adaptation** of a book or a play.

In a screenplay, the words have a special place on the page.

Read on to see how a portion of a screenplay might appear. Hort and Tilly are my wacky characters. They'll slip us some fun information about writing too.

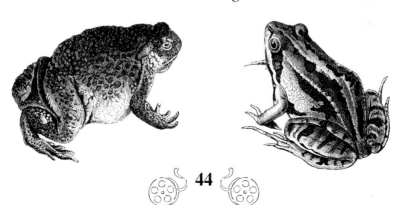

TILLY

Well, you sure look bug-eyed. Like you're going to croak.

HORT

I'm not croaking. I'm straining to see where we are. Perhaps we're in a movie!

TILLY

Well, where are all the cameras? By the way, I think you're in my light, Dort.

HORT

My name is Hort. And there aren't any movie cameras yet. We're trapped in the writing of this screenplay. Look. Whatever we say ends up on this page.

TILLY

Well, I'll be a squirrel's aunt. You're right. So, what should we do? Hey, maybe we can say anything we want. After all, this is our movie.

HORT

Be very careful here. Perhaps people are reading what we're saying.

TILLY

That's the fun of it. Let's go for it. Come on. Say something crazy. We know it's a comedy if you're in it. What's the matter? Rat got your tongue?

HORT

First of all, there seems to be plenty of mouth motion coming from you. And it seems I have to wait to speak. I can only talk when the writer says I can.

TILLY

Pretty spooky stuff. But look. Even *this* is getting printed on the page. Hey, I've got an idea. Let's try something different here. What if I do something besides talk?

HORT

Great idea.

TILLY

(Before speaking, Tilly pats her head. And she rubs her stomach. Then Tilly speaks.)

So that's what happens. What we *do* gets typed out in a different way. Hey, what if I say something angrily or very loudly?!

HORT

I wish you wouldn't.

TILLY

(loudly)

I am going to talk very loudly now! Look! There's where you put the word! Right below the name!

And you can put other stuff in there. Like if I'm rising to say it! Or to whom I'm talking! This is fun to create! Come on! Be a sport, Gort!

HORT

The name is Hort. And I wish you had come with volume control. Just remember. We don't create characters. We *are* the characters. The writer plugs in her imagination. And she actually gets to write our *dialogue!* That means she will decide what we say. Why should she have all the fun?

TILLY

Give the screenwriter a little slack. She's made up interesting characters here. And people won't be able to figure out what we're going to say next. That means we aren't *predictable.* All of that is important in a screenplay. And we don't always get along.

HORT

Yes, that's part of the scheme too. That's one way to make **conflict** in the movies. By having two very different kinds of characters interact with each other. And conflict is important in a screenplay. Otherwise, it's quite boring. So even our personalities are all a part of *her* goal. Can't you see that?

TILLY

Well, we're different all right! At least one of us is anyway.

HORT
(angrily)

I'm not absorbing your utterings, Tilly the Silly. It's all the writer's design to get us to argue. I want out of this movie script. I've had enough. So the screenwriter wants conflict. I'll give her conflict. I'm leaving. I want off this page. *Now!*

TILLY

Wait a minute. Did you ever think about this? What if the writer stops thinking about us? If she thinks this script isn't working right, she'll—

HORT
(worriedly)

She'll what?

TILLY

I can't say it. It's too horrible.

HORT

Just say it!

TILLY

The writer will push "delete" on her computer! And then we'll just disappear!

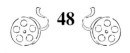

HORT

No! I hadn't even thought of that. That *is* terrible!

TILLY

Maybe we should be grateful for what we have.

HORT

What *do* we have?

TILLY

We have each other. We can learn to make the best of it.

HORT

Do we have to? Remember, not all movies have happy endings.

TILLY

Well, *this* one does. So you'd better start seeing some friendship possibilities between us.

HORT

You mean you could be friends with someone like me?

TILLY

I could try. I do like your name. It rhymes with wart.

HORT

So is this the end of the screenplay? Now that the conflict is over?

TILLY

Not at all. But it's the end of this chapter.

HORT
(warmly)

And the beginning of a wonderful friendship?

TILLY
(sincerely)

You say such goofy things, Mort.

HORT

The name is Hort.

How About a Movie Party?

Want to treat your friends to a movie? And not spend a lot of money? Why don't you have a movie party? You could organize it. And then invite your friends. Have a parent help you serve soda and popcorn to your guests.

Also, make sure the movie you rent is parent-approved. Then roll 'em!

After the movie, talk about it. See what your friends think about the movie.

Here are some fun discovery questions for you all to think about.

- Did you think the movie was good or bad? Why did you think that?
- What was your favorite part in the movie?
- What part did you dislike?
- What do you think the movie was really about?
- On a scale from 1 to 10, how did it rate?
- Does the movie have a book to go with it? If it does, has anyone read it? How does the book compare to the movie?
- Would you recommend this movie to other friends?
- What is your favorite movie of all time?
- What makes it special?

Did your friends enjoy themselves? Then why not create your own movie club? Meet once a month or so to watch and discuss movies.

Maybe next time, you could try something different. Check out a classic black-and-white movie. Or maybe even a foreign film.

And don't forget the popcorn!

It's a Wrap

In movie jargon, "It's a wrap!" means, "We're finished!"

I hope you've had some fun looking inside the movie business.

By the way, this author likes going to the movies. I especially enjoy romantic comedies and some foreign films. But one of my favorite movies is *Chariots of Fire*. It won an Academy Award for best picture in 1981.

What types of films do you like the most? Do you like westerns, comedies, or science fiction? There are so many to choose from.

Here's an idea— Make a list of all your favorite movies. Then turn that list into a bookmark. Share this book and your bookmark with your friends. Let them in on all your movie discoveries.

In the meantime— Have fun at the movies!

GLOSSARY

Academy Award   a major award in the film industry. It's also known as an Oscar.

adaptation   a movie script that's based on another work, such as a book or a play

agent   a person who helps a performer find work

animate   to bring to life or create movement

audition   a tryout

backup   background singing

block   to do a rough practice version of a scene

casting   assigning parts to actors

classical   a traditional form of music that includes chamber music, opera, and symphony

clique   an exclusive circle of close friends

competitive   to really want to come out on top, as in winning a game, a prize, or a job

conflict   opposing forces, such as people or events, that add interest to the drama of a story

consultant   one who offers professional advice on a specific topic to other people and businesses

contacts   people in similar fields of work who may be able to help each other

contract   a legal agreement

demo	short for *demonstration*
discipline	the ability to focus on the task at hand
documentary	a type of film that explores real events
Grammy	a major award in the music industry
illusion	a special effect that tricks the viewer into seeing something that's not there
mythical	imaginary. Also, people, animals, and situations found in myths.
octave	a group of eight musical notes
prehistoric	something that existed before recorded history
prop	short for property; a single item used in a film, such as a fake gun
score	the music for a movie
rehearsal	a practice
résumé	a summary of a person's work history
role	an actor's part in a movie—the person they portray
talent	natural ability
technical	relating to a mechanical or scientific subject

Index